Sagarmatha
Climbing Mount Everest

Ben Nussbaum

Consultant
Jamey Acosta, M.S.Ed.
Reading Specialist and English Learner TOSA

Publishing Credits
Rachelle Cracchiolo, M.S.Ed., *Publisher*
Emily R. Smith, M.A.Ed., *SVP of Content Development*
Véronique Bos, *VP of Creative*
Dona Herweck Rice, *Senior Content Manager*
Jill Malcolm, *Senior Graphic Designer*

Image Credits: p.5 (middl) Alamy; p.11 NASA; p.14
(bottom) Shutterstock/Storm Is Me; p.15 Shutterstock/
sihasakprachum; p.15 Shutterstock/sihasakprachum; p.17
(Middle) Alamy/Royal Geographical Society; p.18 iStock/
fotoVoyager; p.19 (top) Alamy/SuperStock; p.19 (bottom)
Getty/DEVENDRA M SINGH; p.20 iStock/sihasakprachum;
p.21 (middle) iStock/mkitina4; p.21 (bottom) Shutterstock/
O'SHI; p.22 Getty/NAMGYAL SHERPA; p.23 Shutterstock/T.
Schneider; p.26 (middle) Getty/Royal Geographical Society;
p.27 (middle) Getty/NISHA BHANDARI; all other images
from iStock or Shutterstock

**Library of Congress Cataloging in Publication Control
Number:** 2024041793

TCM Teacher Created Materials

5482 Argosy Avenue
Huntington Beach, CA 92649
www.tcmpub.com
ISBN 979-8-7659-9551-8

Table of Contents

The Highest Peak

A massive and majestic mountain **range** marks the border between China and Nepal. This range is the Himalayas. Many of the tallest mountains in the world are staggered along this range. These mountains are hard to get to and are covered in snow. Yet, for climbers around the world, they are a thrilling challenge, and the drive to climb them is **legendary**.

Sagarmatha is the tallest of all the mountains in the Himalayas. In fact, it is the highest mountain in the world—and therefore, the highest **elevation** of anything on Earth. Nothing humans have made comes anywhere close to Sagarmatha's staggering height.

That's Tall!

Sagarmatha is about 8,848 meters (29,032 feet) in elevation. The tallest mountain in the United States is Denali, which is about 6,190 meters (20,310 feet) high.

Sagarmatha is known by many names. The name *Sagarmatha* comes from Nepal and means **"peak** of heaven." In Tibet, the peak is called *Chomolungma*. This means "goddess mother of the world." Both names signify the respect that people give to the mountain. In the United States and Great Britain, Sagarmatha has long been known as Mount Everest. The English people named it *Everest* after Sir George Everest of England, who was the **surveyor general** of India.

Everest is usually pronounced EH-ver-est, but Sir George Everest's name is correctly pronounced EVE-rest.

Climbing Sagarmatha is dangerous and expensive. It also takes a great deal of time and patience. Climbers spend about two months slowly moving up the icy giant. Even the most experienced climbers need some luck to make this happen. They need to stay healthy and injury-free, which is challenging given the conditions they are in. They also need luck as far as the weather goes, because a big storm can completely **derail** their climb. Likewise, avalanches are a constant threat. It takes much more than simple determination to successfully climb Sagarmatha!

Climbers who reach the peak of Sagarmatha cannot stay there for long. It is not a safe place to relax. But for a short moment, they get to celebrate. They smile, wave flags, take pictures, or shoot short videos from the top of the world. Then, they make another strenuous trek back down the mountain.

Even the most skilled climbers take many weeks to climb Sagarmatha. It takes about 10 to 15 days just to reach the mountain base to begin the climb!

Sagarmatha

Lhotse

Hi, Neighbor!

Lhotse is the fourth-tallest mountain in the world. The peak of Lhotse is only about 3 kilometers (2 miles) away from the peak of Sagarmatha.

Climbers attempt to scale Sagarmatha.

The Geography of Sagarmatha

Sagarmatha was formed by movements of plates in Earth's crust. The plates converged, or collided, causing one plate to move upward and the other downward. The towering mountain range that resulted is marked by peaks, valleys, and glaciers.

Some of the most common rocks found within Sagarmatha are granite, limestone, and schist. However, not much rock is seen because the entire summit of the mountain is covered by packed and frozen snow. This snow is hard as a rock. It is covered by a thick layer of soft snow.

Climbers walk across a glacier as they climb Sagarmatha.

Yaks

Yaks are common pack animals on Sagarmatha. They have very thick fur to keep them warm. Their lungs are large, allowing them to breathe in the **thin air**. Yaks can carry about 100 kilograms (220 pounds) of supplies while climbing near the base of the mountain.

There is very little plant life on Sagarmatha. Moss grows to about two-thirds up the mountain. That moss is thought to be the highest-**altitude** plant in the world. A small, jumping spider can be found up to about this same height. A type of goose may even fly to the mountain's summit. A few mammals live in the mountain's lower elevations. Even though Sagarmatha is extremely cold and the air is thin, there is still life on the mountain.

moss and lichen

A Hard Climb

Sagarmatha is not a very **steep** mountain. People can make it to the top even if they don't have great climbing skills. But, reaching the peak is still very hard. In fact, it can be deadly.

The main challenge climbers have is that Sagarmatha is so high in the air. The Willis Tower is a famous **skyscraper** in Chicago. It is 110 stories tall. For many years, the Willis Tower was the tallest building in the world. But, the Willis Tower would be like a bug at your feet in comparison. It would take about 20 Willis Towers stacked on top of each other to meet Sagarmatha "eye to eye"!

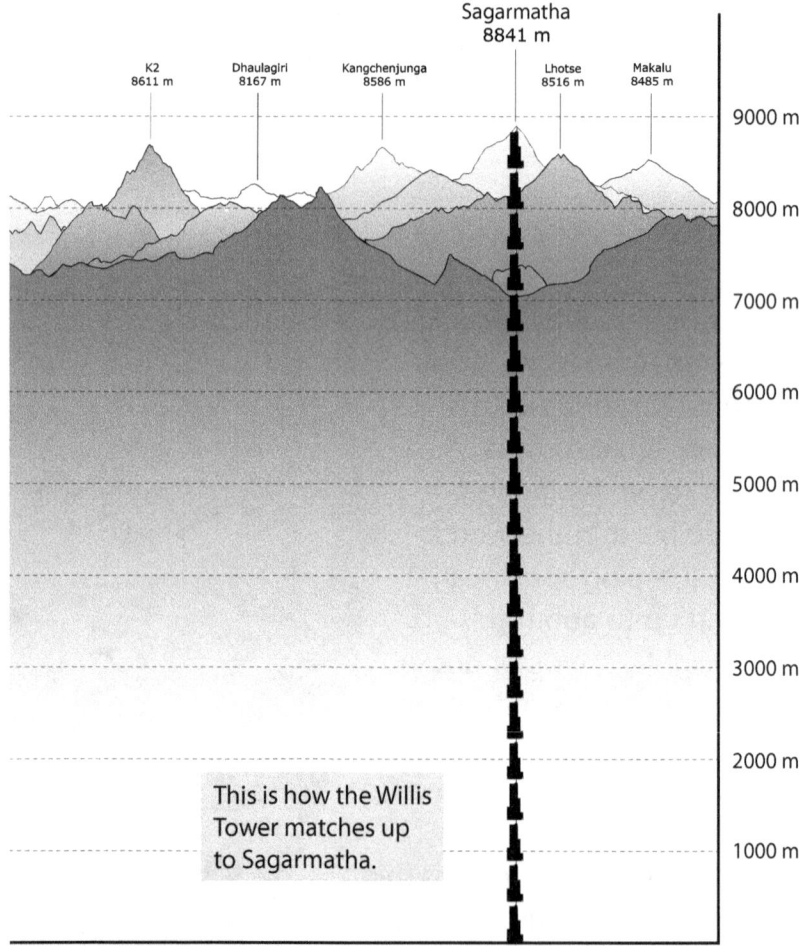

Sagarmatha
8841 m

K2
8611 m

Dhaulagiri
8167 m

Kangchenjunga
8586 m

Lhotse
8516 m

Makalu
8485 m

9000 m

8000 m

7000 m

6000 m

5000 m

4000 m

3000 m

2000 m

1000 m

This is how the Willis Tower matches up to Sagarmatha.

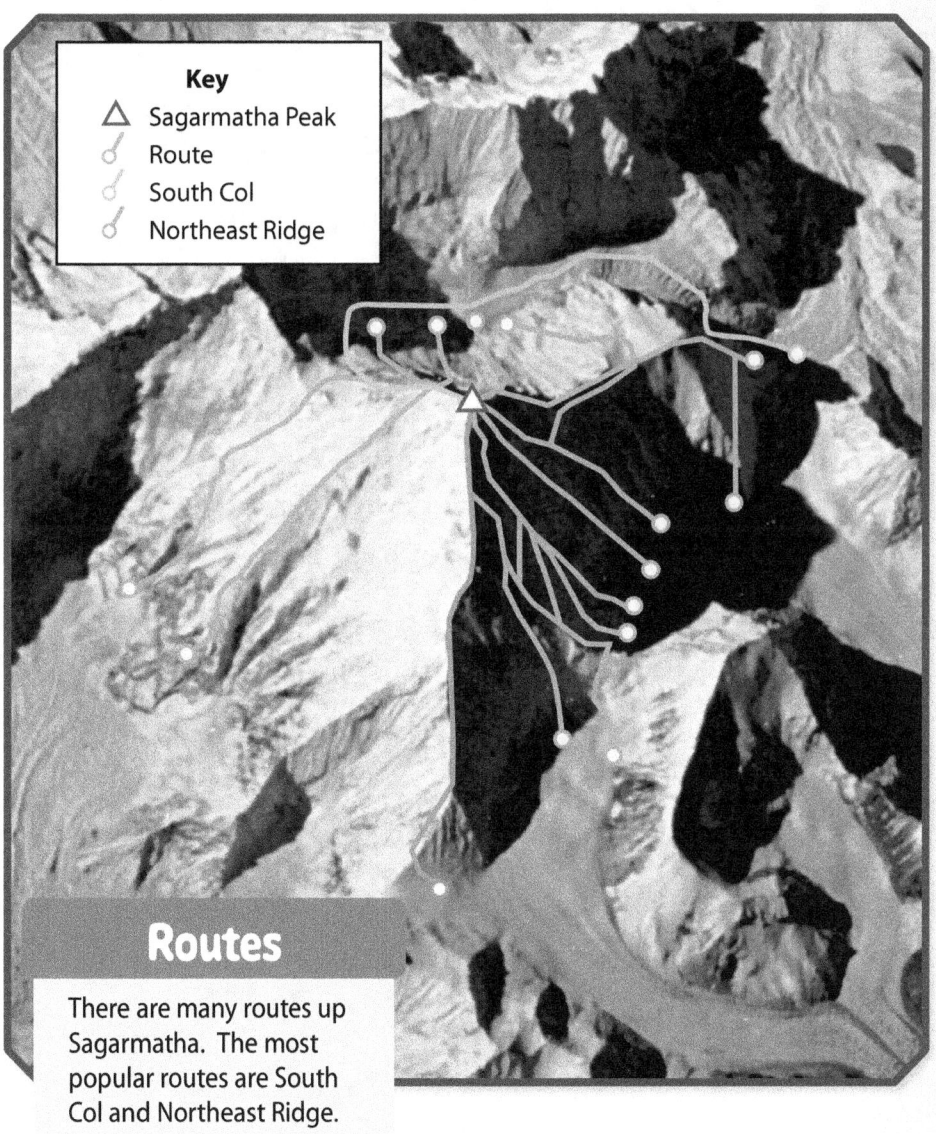

Key
△ Sagarmatha Peak
⚲ Route
⚲ South Col
⚲ Northeast Ridge

Routes

There are many routes up Sagarmatha. The most popular routes are South Col and Northeast Ridge.

This is the challenge for people climbing to Sagarmatha's heights. That high up, the air is not the same as what people are used to, even when they live in high elevations. The air on Sagarmatha is known as thin air. Thin air does not hold heat well; therefore, Sagarmatha is always freezing cold. Even in the summer, temperatures can fall below –18 °C (0 °F). And, low temperatures also mean plenty of snow and ice. Deep snow is very hard to walk in, and ice can easily cause accidents.

Another way that air changes at high elevations is that it has less **oxygen**. Human lungs breathe in oxygen. Then, blood takes the oxygen throughout the body.

People become tired if they don't have enough oxygen. They get confused, and they may start sweating and coughing. Eventually, they faint and then may die.

One way people solve the oxygen problem is to pause their climbing for days or even weeks while on Sagarmatha. Climbers stay in camps high on the mountain. These camps are not very comfortable. Climbers are cold, and they can get bored. But, taking a break in a camp lets the climbers get used to the thin air. It takes some time for the body to adjust.

Hikers take shelter at Sagarmatha base camp.

Climbers also bring tanks of oxygen with them. They breathe this oxygen through a mask, as a scuba diver would. But, climbers still don't have as much oxygen as they need and use in normal conditions. Because of this, their minds and bodies slow down. This, of course, can pose great health risks.

Making the Climb Even Harder

Some people have made it to the top of Sagarmatha without using oxygen from a tank, but it is very rare. Each year, only a few climbers even attempt this.

The thin air causes other problems, too. Lungs can fill with **fluid**, and brains can **swell**. Blood becomes thicker. Heart problems are common.

Each person's body responds in a different way to the thin air. It is hard to predict what will happen when a person spends time at a very high elevation.

If a person does have a medical problem, getting help is very difficult. Even if there are doctors nearby, they do not have their normal equipment. The air is too thin for helicopters to fly, and there are no roads up the mountain. The only way down is to climb or be carried.

A climber rests while feeling the effects of elevation on her body.

An injured climber is carried down Sagarmatha.

Climbers must carry everything they need as they scale the mountain.

On Sagarmatha, anything that would normally be a little problem becomes a huge problem. This is another reason why climbing the mountain is so difficult—because everything is a challenge! There are no stores. It is impossible to spend a night in a hotel. Each bite of food has to be carried up the mountain in someone's pack. If supplies are damaged or lost, nothing can be done about it.

Death on Sagarmatha

Through the years, about 330 people are known to have died on Sagarmatha. Many of those bodies have been left on the mountainside because of the risks to those who would need to carry them out.

Another challenge in climbing Sagarmatha is that the mountain can be crowded. Every year, more and more people from all around the world attempt to climb the peak. But, there are limited paths up Sagarmatha, and, at times, these paths can be especially narrow. Sometimes, there is a ladder that must be climbed or walked across, but there is room for only one person at a time to do it. This can mean climbers must patiently wait their turn. Waiting is no big deal—normally. But on Sagarmatha, waiting is different. Each minute on the mountain is hard, and one minute of waiting can be one minute too long.

Ladders such as this one can be used to cross mountain gaps.

Climbers on the mountain also have to worry about storms or if it is getting dark. It is hard to endure these things. Climbers must think about how much energy they have and how far they can push their bodies. If they are near the top, they need to make sure they have enough oxygen in their tanks to survive for the rest of the trip up *and* the trip down. A long wait can mean having to give up the climb and turn around because a climber does not have enough of the supplies they would need.

climbers at a Sagarmatha base camp during a storm

Summit Windows

Most climbers try for the summit during April and May. They also may climb during a short window in September and October. These times are known as the "summit windows." Other times of the year are too cold, wet, and windy, with sub-zero temperatures, monsoon rains, and massive winds.

A Team Effort

Climbing Sagarmatha is hard—and that's why it takes a team to do it. Everyone on the mountain has help from someone else.

A lot of that help comes from Sherpa. The Sherpa people have lived near the mountain for hundreds of years. They do not have their own country, but Sherpa have their own traditions and language.

On Sagarmatha, Sherpa are guides. They help carry supplies, cook, and even clean so climbers can save their energy. In an emergency, Sherpa help with rescues.

Many Sherpa work on Sagarmatha year after year. They are brave and skilled climbers. They understand the mountain, and they understand better than anyone what is safe.

A Sherpa carries a heavy expedition load across a glacier.

Sherpa are paid a few thousand dollars for their work each climbing season. With the money they make from climbing, they can support their families. But they do not get rich, and their work is very dangerous. In 2014, 16 Sherpa died in an avalanche.

Perhaps the most famous Sherpa is Tenzing Norgay. He and Edmund Hillary of New Zealand were the first two people to climb to the peak of Sagarmatha. They achieved this feat in 1953, and it took them 16 days to make the climb.

Edmund Hillary and Tenzing Norgay

Wedding on High

In 2005, a Sherpa named Pem Dorjee and a climber named Moni Mulepati were married at the top of Sagarmatha. They chose to get married there because their different religions did not support them being married. So, they decided to get married someplace where no one could tell them what to do!

Other people who are not Sherpa also work as guides. These guides live in the United States, Europe, Japan, and other places. They run companies that specialize in helping people climb Sagarmatha and other famous mountains. They work with groups who are making the climb. A guide might have five or six climbers at a time. The climbers become a team, and they support one another along the way.

These guides help people with each step of the **process**. They help them buy the right gear, tickets, and **permits**. Climbers are required to have permits to climb the mountain. The guides also make sure the climbing group has enough food, oxygen, and other supplies.

Climbers prepare necessary equipment for their journey.

Guides stay with their climbers all the way up Sagarmatha. Some guides have reached the peak ten or more times. Sometimes, climbers who are sick or weak want to keep going. Their guide assesses the situation and tells them if it is not safe to keep going. Even at the top of the mountain, guides must always think clearly. Climbers put their lives in their guide's hands.

Interested climbers must secure and validate the right permits.

Permits to Climb

As of 2025, a single permit to climb Sagarmatha is about $15,000. A climber can only be granted a permit to climb Sagarmatha if they have already climbed another mountain in Nepal that is over 6,500 meters (21,325 feet).

Helping Sagarmatha

Even though Sagarmatha is the highest mountain on Earth, it is fragile in some ways. One problem is that too many people have left too much **litter** on it. Litter is damaging to the environment.

A lot of the trash left behind is empty oxygen tanks. These tanks are heavy and awkward. It is tempting to toss them into the snow once they're empty. Food wrappers, cooking stoves, and even broken tents are other types of trash. Some trash is left behind because of emergencies on the mountain. When climbers are trying to stay alive, they are not as worried about picking up their things. Other times, people are simply trying to drop weight or make their climb more comfortable. They do not always think about the environment or their effect on it.

Left-behind trash has become a big challenge on the mountain.

Sherpa and the government of Nepal are working together to clean the mountain. Some Sherpa climb the mountain just to collect trash. Companies are helping, too. They pay for trips that collect trash and bring it off the mountain.

Some guides are also helping. They are promising that any group they lead will not leave trash on the mountain. They know how important it is to preserve this special place.

The "Carry Me Back" project attempts to have tourists remove waste from the Sagarmatha area.

Yuck!

A very gross kind of problem on Sagarmatha is poop. The mountain is so cold that poop does not decay as quickly as it normally does down below. So, there is a lot of human poop on the mountain. Climbers are now required to carry special bags for their waste and take it up and down the mountain with them!

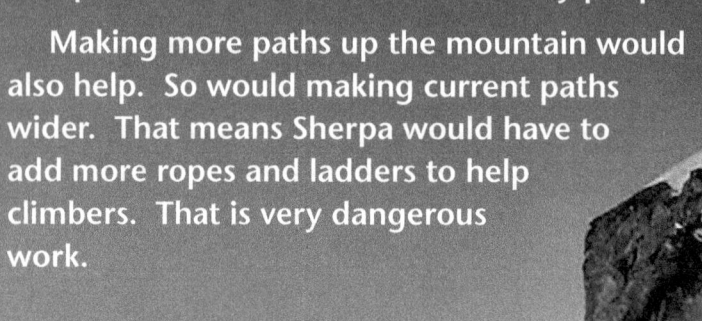

People are trying to solve the problem of overcrowding, too. For example, not just anyone can start climbing Sagarmatha. To help with overcrowding, the government of Nepal could sell fewer permits. Fewer permits would mean fewer climbers. Fewer climbers can help make the mountain a little safer.

But, fewer permits would also mean less money for the government. And if there aren't as many climbers, that means there aren't as many jobs for guides and Sherpa. This is the livelihood for many people.

Making more paths up the mountain would also help. So would making current paths wider. That means Sherpa would have to add more ropes and ladders to help climbers. That is very dangerous work.

Let's Give It a Go!

About 800 people a year decide to do just that—give the climb a go. About 30 to 50 percent of all climbs are successful.

And then, some people are worried about making it too easy to climb Sagarmatha. Adding too many ladders makes the mountain less wild and less of a challenge. The equipment also makes the mountain less beautiful.

There are no easy answers, but many climbers insist it is important to find a solution.

People line up to reach the peak of Sagarmatha in the same way they might line up for an amusement park ride.

An Amazing Accomplishment

A man named George Mallory was one of the first people to try to climb Sagarmatha, although he never made it to the top. People all over the world knew his name. They read about his adventures in newspapers. Someone asked him why he wanted to climb the mountain. Mallory's response is famous. He said, "Because it's there." Mallory died on Sagarmatha during his last attempt.

Climbers are constantly **drawn** to the challenge of Sagarmatha. They feel a need to conquer the mountain, even if climbing it is hard, dangerous, and expensive. People will always want to get to the top of the tallest mountain in the world.

George Mallory

Each year, only a few hundred people in the entire world make it to the top of Sagarmatha. For the rest of their lives, they can say they are part of a tiny club. They can show people photos. They can tell stories, and they can share incredible memories of their time at the peak of this majestic mountain.

For the Record

A Nepali Sherpa named Kami Rita holds the record for climbing Sagarmatha the most. By early 2024, he had reached its peak 30 times.

Sagarmatha peak

Think Like a Scientist

Freezing temperatures are a key factor in visiting Sagarmatha. You can learn about the rate at which water freezes and how different substances affect it by doing an experiment like this.

What to Get

- 5 identical plastic cups (clear is best)
- permanent marker
- large pitcher filled with room-temperature water
- measuring cup
- 1 tbsp. salt
- 1 tbsp. sugar
- 1 tbsp. flour
- 1 tbsp. soil
- 5 mixing spoons or stirrers
- freezer
- timer
- paper and pen

What to Do

1 Label each of the five cups with one of these labels: water, salt, sugar, flour, soil.

2 Pour water from the pitcher into each cup, filling it with the exact same amount (about half full). You can use a measuring cup to ensure the amount of water in each cup is exactly the same. Pouring water from the pitcher also ensures the water in each cup is the same temperature.

3 Do nothing with the cup marked "water." With each of the other cups, add one tablespoon of the named item to the water. Stir the item into the water, using a different spoon for each cup. In this way, you can ensure the items do not cross-contaminate other cups.

4 Place all five cups on the same shelf in the freezer, side by side. Close the freezer.

5 Set the timer for 20 minutes. After 20 minutes, open the freezer and note quick observations about the water in each cup. Close the freezer. Set the timer for another 20 minutes.

6 At the next 20-minute mark, record observations and set the timer again. Continue until all cups of water have frozen.

7 What do you notice about the time it takes for each cup to freeze? Which cup freezes first? Which freezes last? What can you conclude about water's freezing point as affected by other substances?

Glossary

altitude—height or elevation

derail—throw off track

drawn—pulled toward something

elevation—the height of a place

fluid—a substance that can flow freely, such as water

legendary—very famous and well known

litter—trash left in places it should not be

oxygen—a chemical that is found in air and is necessary for humans to breathe

peak—the highest point

permits—legal permissions to do something

process—the steps involved in doing something

range—a group of mountains

skyscraper—a very tall building made of many floors

steep—almost straight up and down

surveyor general—government official who is in charge of measuring and mapping land and its boundaries

swell—increase in size

thin air—atmosphere that is much less dense and with lower air pressure than at sea level, and therefore harder for living things to breathe

Index

Your Turn

On Sagarmatha, people get incredibly tired. Each step takes a lot of effort, and they become exhausted. Can you recall a time when you were fully exhausted? What had you been doing to make you so tired? Draw a picture of and write a descriptive journal entry about this moment in your life.

www.ingramcontent.com/pod-product-compliance
Lightning Source LLC
Chambersburg PA
CBHW061723120626
46550CB00003B/1336